GET YOUR DEUTSCH ON!

Θ

THERAN PRESS

THERAN PRESS IS THE ACADEMIC PUBLISHING IMPRINT OF SILVER GOAT MEDIA.

THERAN IS DEDICATED TO AUTHENTIC PARTNERSHIPS WITH OUR ACADEMIC ASSOCIATES, TO THE QUALITY DESIGN OF SCHOLARLY BOOKS, AND TO ELITE STANDARDS OF PEER REVIEW.

THERAN SEEKS TO FREE INTELLECTUALS FROM THE CONFINES OF TRADITIONAL PUBLISHING.

THERAN SCHOLARS ARE AUTHORITIES AND REVOLUTIONARIES IN THEIR RESPECTIVE FIELDS.

THERAN ENCOURAGES NEW MODELS FOR GENERATING AND DISTRIBUTING KNOWLEDGE.

FOR OUR CREATIVES, FOR OUR COMMUNITIES, FOR OUR WORLD.

WWW.THERANPRESS.ORG

This book was designed and produced by Silver Goat Media, LLC. Fargo, ND U.S.A.
www.silvergoatmedia.com
SGM, the SGM goat, Theran Press, and the Theran theta are trademarks of Silver Goat Media, LLC.

Cover design: Travis Klath © 2017 SGM
This book was typeset in Oswald and Palatino Linotype by Aurora McClain and Cady Ann Mittlestadt.

A portion of the annual proceeds from the sale of this book is donated to the Longspur Prairie Fund.
www.longspurprairie.org

ISBN-10:1-944296-10-7
ISBN-13:978-1-944296-10-0

Printed and bound in the United States of America.

GET YOUR DEUTSCH ON!

Basic German in Two Weeks

Thomas C. Mayer

THERAN PRESS

„Wer fremde Sprachen nicht kennt, weiß nichts von seiner eigenen."
Johann Wolfgang von Goethe

Introduction

This book is designed to introduce you to some of the basic principles of modern German. While it's not a "pocket phrase book" or a "vocabulary book," it is an ideal text for the serious student, traveler, and explorer searching for a fast introduction to one of the most glorious languages in the world. This book is also intended to get you talking with your new German colleagues, neighbors, and friends as quickly as possible. Finally, this book is meant to be fun. We all learned our first language when we were children. That's a fact worth keeping in mind. In a way, learning another language asks that you become a child again and that you do things children do all the time: that you enjoy yourself without fear, that you make mistakes without worry, and that you play. If you can do that, if you play with the material that I've put together for you in this little book, then you can learn some basic German and you'll have fun doing it.

This book is the second in a new series of introductory language textbooks published by Theran Press. The first—*Get Your Greek On!*—was written by Dr. Peter Schultz, an old friend of mine. The series blurs the traditional boundary between a tourist's phrase book and a traditional language textbook. While you'll find key phrases and vocabularies here, you'll also find a healthy dose of basic grammar that will allow you to understand how German actually works. The goal is for you to learn enough German to get around, to meet people, and to more fully enjoy yourself during your time in Germany or in other German-speaking nations.

My passion for German began in 1981—at the age of nine—when I attended Concordia College's German language summer immersion camp, Waldsee. For the next five summers I went back to Waldsee, studied German in Junior High and High School, completed a degree in German at Concordia College, and eventually ended up living and working in Germany. Writing this book is my way to give back, to share with you the love and passion I've had for the German language these past 36 years.

Producing a book—even a tiny one like this—is always a team effort. In that spirit, it's a pleasure to offer thanks to Mike Cushman, Sheila Cushman, Carol Keelan, Chris Keelan, Peter Schultz, and Nicola Wood for their comments and criticism. Three virtuosi—Travis Klath, Aurora McClain, and Cady Ann Mittlestadt—generated the book's cover, interior production values, and design. Special thanks to Brad Ruff and Neil Souther for their inspirational language teaching. If you find an error, or would like to offer a suggestion for the next edition of *Get Your Deutsch On!*, please do let me know: info@silvergoatmedia.com.

How to Use This Book

The most important thing that you can do when beginning to learn another language is to play with it. That's what counts. Right now, it doesn't matter if you sound like a gibbering lunatic when you speak German. It doesn't matter if you can't spell a single word when you write German. It doesn't matter if you don't understand the grammar when you read German. Right now, what matters is that you *try* to speak, that you *try* to write, and that you *try* to read. At these earliest stages, when you're just dipping your toe in the water, the most important thing you can do is to play with the sounds, the words, the phrases, and the grammar that you're trying to learn. Right now, having fun—playing with your German—is what counts.

This book is divided into two parts. Part One provides fourteen lessons. Each of these lessons includes an introduction to some basic parts of German grammar, a set of essential words, phrases, and conversational patterns, and a quiz outline that you can use to "Get Your Deutsch On!" Part Two consists of short German-English and English-German glossaries.

It's important to keep in mind that this book is not a comprehensive German language course, nor is it a "German phrase book." Rather, it's intended to be a very quick, very simple introduction to a few of the most *basic* principles of German for the student, traveler, or explorer. Moreover, while this book will be of use for those who want to learn German on their own, it will be far more effective when integrated into an active, playful, classroom environment. In language instruction, there's no substitute for a great teacher. And having just one other playmate can make your experience much more meaningful and much more fun. If you want to "Get Your Deutsch On!" there's no better way than with an enthusiastic instructor and crew of fun friends.

If you want to move beyond this book's rather basic functions—to increase your grammatical skills, to refine your vocabulary, and to enhance your expressive range—then you'll need to swim into deeper seas. Fortunately, many good guides exist that can help speed you on your way. For these, take a look at the Further Reading section at the end of this book.

Now, stop reading this English! Go Get Your Deutsch On!

Part One. The Lessons

Lesson 1

Essential Grammar

1.1 The Alphabet

A	a	**ah**, as in "**Ah** ha!"
B	b	**bay**
C	c	**tsay**
D	d	**day**
E	e	**ay,** as in "**day**"
F	f	**eff** *(same as English)*
G	g	**gay**
H	h	**ha**, as in "Ah **ha**!"
I	i	**e**, as in **e**-mail
J	j	**yot**
K	k	**ka** *(like the British English for "car")*
L	l	**ell** *(same as English)*
M	m	**em** *(same as English)*
N	n	**en** *(same as English)*
O	o	**oh** *(same as American English)*
P	p	**pay**
Q	q	**coo**, as in chicken **coo**p
R	r	**air**
S	s	**es** *(same as English)*
T	t	**tay**
U	u	**oo**, as in **zoo**
V	v	**fow**, as in **f+ow** as in w**ow**
W	w	**vay**
X	x	**icks**
Y	y	**oop-see-lon**
Z	z	**tset**, as in **t+set** the table
Ä	ä	**eh**
Ö	ö	**oe**
Ü	ü	**ue**
ß		**esstset** *(Note: we will use "***ss***" instead of "***ß***" throughout this book, which is what the Swiss do)*

1.2 The Sounds the Letters Make

Now that you know how to say the alphabet, let's look at the sounds the letters make when they are in words. Many are similar to English.

A	**ah**, as in "**Ah** ha!"
B	**b**, as in **b**ear
C	**k**, as in **k**ick
D	**d**, as in **d**ay; *when at end of word,***t** as in ba**t**
E	**ay**, as "**h**ay"
F	**f**, as in **f**ine
G	**g**, as in **g**roup; *when at end of word,***k** as in **k**ick
H	**h**, as in **h**ello
I	**i**, as in **i**gloo
J	**y**, as in **y**awn
K	**k**, as in **k**ick
L	**l**, as in **l**ong
M	**m**, as in **m**an
N	**n**, as in **m**an
O	**o**, as in **o**pen
P	**p**, as in **p**ay
Q	**k**, as in **k**ick
R	**r**, as in **r**aisin
S	**z**, as in **z**oo; *when at beginning of word, otherwise* **s**, as in **s**afe
T	**t**, as in **s**et; *though perhaps a bit more energetic!*
U	**oo**, as in **z**oo; **u**, as in p**u**t
V	**f**, as in **f**ast; *in most cases; sometimes* **v**, as in **v**itamin
W	**v**, as in **v**itamin
X	**cks**, as in ti**cks**
Y	**ü** (*like* **ü** *below, but shorter*)
Z	**ts**, as in dar**ts**
Ä	**eh**, as in "**Meh**!" (*think Dilbert*)
Ö	**oe** (*shape your mouth as if to say "oh!" but say "ee" instead*)
Ü	**ue** (*shape your mouth as if to say "ooh!" but say "ee" instead*)
ß	**s**, as in **s**afe; *though a bit more drawn out*

1.3 Some Essential Sounds Comprised of a Couple Letters

au	**ow**, as in "**Ow**! That hurts!"
äu	**oi**, as in **oi**l
ch	Search YouTube for "How to pronounce **CH** in German."
ck	**k**, as in **k**ick
dt	**t**, as in **s**et
ee	**ay**, as in **d**ay
ei	**I**, as in "**I** am."
eu	**oi**, as in **oi**l
ie	**ee**, as in scr**ee**ch
ig	**ich** (*see* ch *above*)

pf	**pf** *(not present in English)*
ph	**f**, as in **f**un
qu	**kv** *(not present in English)*
sch	**sh**, as in **sh**ut
sp	**shp** *(not present in English)*
st	**sht** *(not present in English)*
tsch	**ch**, as in **ch**owder
zsch	**ch**, as in **ch**owder
tz	**ts**, as in pan**ts**

1.4 Letter Sounds and Syllables

German is a phonetic language, which means the letters and letter combinations in words almost always make the same sounds, with exceptions limited mainly to foreign words. You won't have to grapple with silent letters or weird exceptions. What you have above is essentially all you will ever need to pronounce German.

Essential Phrases and Vocabulary

Hallo! / Tschüss!	*Hello! / Goodbye!*
Bitte! / Danke!	*Please! / Thank you!*
Ja! / Nein!	*Yes! / No!*
Wie heisst du?	*What is your name?*
Ich heisse Peter.	*My name is Peter.*
Wie schreibt man X?	*How do you spell X?*
Wie sagt man X auf Deutsch?	*How do you say X in German?*

If you want to Get Your Deutsch On . . .

– You will know all the letters of the German alphabet and you will be able to pronounce them correctly and know the sounds they make. Play with the letters!

– MOST IMPORTANTLY! You will be able to understand and pronounce all essential phrases and vocabulary from Lesson 1.

Lesson 2

Essential Grammar

2.1 Nouns and Gender

A noun is a person, place, or thing. German nouns differ from English nouns in that they have specific genders. They can be *masculine, feminine,* or *neuter,* as indicated by the words **der, die,** or **das.**

der Mann	*the man*	(*masculine*)
die Frau	*the woman*	(*feminine*)
das Haus	*the house*	(*neuter*)

The concept of nouns having different genders can be confusing for those new to the German language. In some cases, the gender is intuitive, as with the example of **der Mann** and **die Frau**. Unfortunately, however, the gender of most German words is not intuitive. There are endless rules and rules of thumb for determining the gender of German nouns. For example, all German nouns ending in **-chen** or **-lein** are **das**. For beginners, however, it is perhaps easiest to think of the gender as an integral part of any noun and to learn it together with the noun itself. For example, think of the German word for *house* as **das Haus** rather than just **Haus**.

Also, don't get too caught up with gender when you're speaking German. It has little bearing on your ability to make yourself understood, and even German native speakers occasionally make mistakes.

2.2 Definite and Indefinite Articles

Articles help us explain whether a noun we are talking about is specific or general in nature—e.g. "the house" vs. "a house." When we are talking about a specific noun, we use the word *the* in English. It is called a "definite article." German has three definite articles, i.e. three ways of saying *the:* **der, die,** or **das**, depending on the gender of the noun.

When we're talking about a general noun, we use the words *a* or *an* in English. These are called "indefinite articles." The corresponding German word is **ein** or **eine**, depending on the gender of the noun in question.

der Mann *the man* (*masculine*)
ein Mann *a man*

die Frau *the woman* (*feminine*)
eine Frau *a woman*

das Haus *the house* (*neuter*)
ein Haus *a house*

2.3 Singular and Plural

In English we generally add *-s* or *-es* to make nouns plural. In German there are many different plural endings. Some of the common ones include **-n, -en, -e, -s, -r**, and **-er**. Some plural endings don't change at all. Regardless of the change in ending, the definite article of all plural nouns changes to **die**. Here are some examples:

-n	die Katze / die Katzen	*the cat / the cats*
-e	der Wein / die Weine	*the wine / the wines*
-s	das Auto / die Autos	*the car / the cars*
¨er	das Buch / die Bücher	*the book / the books*
No change	das Mädchen / die Mädchen	*the girl / the girls*

As with gender, it's easiest to learn the plural ending when you first learn the noun. However, there are a few rules of thumb which can be helpful:

- Most masculine and neuter plurals add ¨e or **e**.
- Almost all masculine and feminine nouns ending in **-e** add **-n** in the plural.
- All feminine nouns ending in **-heit**, **-keit**, **-schaft**, and **-ung** add **-en** in the plural.

2.4 Cultural Etiquette

Punctuality: Punctuality is a big deal in Germany, Austria, and Switzerland. You're expected to be on time. There is no implicit grace period built into invitations. For example, if someone invites you over to their house at 7:00 p.m., you should be there at 7:00 p.m. and not at 7:30 p.m.

Paying and tipping: In most places you pay your server directly. If you want to leave a tip, it is common to round up to the next whole number (e.g. if the bill were €23.30, you would round up to €24.00). Make sure you give your tip directly to the server. Do not leave it on the table or they may well think you forgot the money there and come running after you.

Lining up / queueing: Austrians, Germans, and the Swiss do not form what North Americans and people from the British Isles would think of as orderly lines / queues. For example, if you go to the bakery, it's up to you to make a mental note of when it's your turn and to speak up promptly when they ask "Who's next?" You may even have to physically position yourself in front of people. The process might feel a bit aggressive at first, but no one means it that way and it's important not to take it personally. Just go with the flow.

Essential Phrases and Vocabulary

Sprechen Sie Englisch?	*Do you speak English?*
Ich spreche Deutsch.	*I speak German.*
Ich spreche kein Englisch / Deutsch.	*I don't speak English / German.*
Woher kommen Sie?	*Where are you from?*
Ich komme aus Kanada / England.	*I am from Canada / England.*
Herzlich willkommen!	*Welcome!*

If you want to Get Your Deutsch On . . .

– You will know the meaning, the proper pronunciation, gender, and plural of all nouns from Lesson 2.
– MOST IMPORTANTLY! You will know and be able to pronounce all essential phrases and vocabulary from Lessons 1-2.

Lesson 3

Essential Grammar

3.1 The Four Cases

The role a noun plays in a sentence determines its "case." German has four cases: nominative, accusative, dative, and genitive. Each of those cases can change the way a noun and its article looks. This can be a bit confusing at first, because German cases are slightly more complex than English ones.

3.2 The Nominative Case

Every sentence has a subject. The subject is the person, place, or thing in the sentence which is doing whatever is being done.

Das Kind pflückt die Blume.
The child picks the flower.

The child is doing the picking. The child is the subject of the sentence and we say it is in the *nominative case*. You already know the definite and indefinite articles for the nominative case, see above, 2.2.

Nom	*m.*	*n.*	*f.*	*pl.*
def.	**der**	**das**	**die**	**die**
indef.	**ein**	**ein**	**eine**	**keine***

*We use **kein** for the indefinite plural because **ein** / **eine** (*a* / *an*) does not make sense in plural. The German word **kein** means *no* or *none*.

Es gibt keine dummen Fragen.
There are no dumb questions.

3.3 The Accusative Case

Some sentences have direct objects, which is the term for the noun receiving the action of the verb.

Das Kind pflückt die Blume.
The child picks the flower.

The flower is the thing being picked, so the flower is the direct object of the sentence and we say it's in the *accusative case*.

Acc	m.	n.	f.	pl.
def.	<u>den</u>	das	die	die
indef.	<u>einen</u>	ein	eine	keine

Only the masculine form changes in the accusative.

Der Ball ist rot.　　　　**Das Kind wirft <u>den</u> Ball.**
The ball is red.　　　　*The child throws the ball.*

3.4 The Dative Case

The dative case is used for indirect objects. An indirect object is the person, place or thing to or for whom something is given, said, or done.

Das Kind wirft dem Mann den Ball.
The child throws the ball to the man.

The child is doing the throwing, and therefore it is the subject. The ball is the thing being thrown, and therefore it is the direct object. The man is the person to whom the ball is being thrown, and therefore he is the indirect object and in the *dative case.*

Dat	m.	n.	f.	pl.
def.	dem	dem	der	den*
indef.	einem	einem	einer	keinen*

*We add an **-n** to most nouns in the dative plural. There are a few exceptions to this, but adding **-n** is a solid rule of thumb. For example:

The plural of **der Mann** is **die Männer.**

Das Kind wirft den Männer<u>n</u> den Ball.
The child throws the ball to the men.

3.5 The Genitive Case

English mainly shows possession using the apostrophe. German mainly shows possession using the genitive case, which is the fourth and final case for German nouns.

Das ist der Ball <u>des Kindes</u>.
That is the <u>child's</u> ball.

This is how articles change in the genitive:

Gen	m.*	n.*	f.	pl.
def.	des	des	der	der
indef.	eines	eines	einer	keiner

*For genitive masculine and neuter nouns, the noun itself also changes. You add -s or -es to it. To keep things simple, add -es to one-syllable words and to any word ending in an s-sound (e.g. -s, -x, etc.). Otherwise, just add -s.

It is normal for the different cases to be confusing when you first learn German and for you to make lots of mistakes. However, using the wrong case has little or no effect on your ability to make yourself understood, so practice with abandon and don't worry about it.

Essential Phrases and Vocabulary

Entschuldigung!	*Pardon me! Excuse me!*
Was bedeutet "Mensch?"	*What does Mensch mean?*
Verstehen Sie?	*Do you understand?*
Ja, ich verstehe.	*Yes, I understand.*
Nein, ich verstehe nicht.	*No, I don't understand.*

If you want to Get Your Deutsch On . . .

– You will know the meaning, the proper pronunciation, and the gender of all nouns in Lessons 2-3.
– You will know the nominative, accusative, dative, and genitive cases, as well as how definite and indefinite articles change in each case.
– MOST IMPORTANTLY! You will know and be able to pronounce all essential phrases and vocabulary from Lessons 1-3.

Lesson 4

Essential Grammar

4.1 Personal Pronouns in the Nominative

Personal pronouns in German are similar to English.

Singular (sing.)
ich	*I*
du	*you (familiar)*
er, sie, es	*he, she, it*
Sie	*you (formal)*

Plural (pl.)
wir	*we*
ihr / Ihr	*you (familiar) / you (formal)*
sie	*they*

German has different pronouns for *you* singular (**du**) and *you* plural (**ihr**). Some parts of the English speaking world make the same distinction in spoken English. For example, in the South in the United States, you might hear "y'all" and in Glasgow or Northern Ireland, among other places, you might hear "yous" for *you* plural.

4.2 Du and Sie

When addressing each other directly, German speakers use different forms of *you* depending on whether they know someone (familiar, abbreviated as fam.) or not (formal, abbreviated as form.):

Familiar *you*: **du** (sing.) **ihr** (pl.)
Formal *you*: **Sie** (sing.) **Ihr** (pl.)

Wie heisst du?	**Wie heissen Sie?**
What is your name?	*What is your name?*

Rules of thumb:
- Children address each other as **du**.
- Adults address children as **du**.
- Children address adults as **Sie**, except for family.
- Adults who do not know each other, or who are in a formal situation, address each other as **Sie**.

If in doubt, start with **Sie**. A German speaker who wants you to say **du** to them will always tell you:

Sag du zu mir.
Say **du** *to me.*

4.3 Personal Pronouns in the Accusative and Dative

Just like nouns, pronouns change according to whether they are nominative, accusative, or dative.

Nom	Acc	Dat	*English*
ich	mich	mir	*me*
du	dich	dir	*you (fam.)*
er, sie, es	ihn, sie, es	ihm, ihr, ihm	*him, her, it*
Sie	Sie	Ihnen	*you (form.)*
wir	uns	uns	*us*
ihr / Ihr	euch / Euch	euch / Euch	*you (fam. / form.)*
sie	sie	ihnen	*them*

Notice that English has only one pronoun for both accusative and dative cases (i.e. for direct and indirect objects):

I see him. [*him* = direct object]
Ich sehe ihn.

I give him the coffee. [*him* = indirect object]
Ich gebe ihm den Kaffee.

4.4 Saying "it" in German

Unlike English, German doesn't have just one word for *it*. German uses the pronoun that matches the gender of the noun in question:

Der Tisch ist gedeckt. Er ist gedeckt.
The table is set. It is set.

Das Handy ist schwarz. Es ist schwarz.
The mobile phone is black. It is black.

Die Katze ist klein. Sie ist klein.
The cat is small. It is small.

Essential Phrases and Vocabulary

Wie geht's?	*How are you?*
Wie geht's euch?	*How are you (all)?*
Gut.	*Good.*
Schlecht.	*Bad.*
Es geht so.	*So-so.*

eins, zwei, drei, vier, fünf, sechs, sieben, acht, neun, zehn
1, 2, 3, 4, 5, 6, 7, 8, 9, 10...

elf, zwölf, dreizehn, vierzehn, fünfzehn, sechzehn, siebzehn, achtzehn, neunzehn, zwanzig, einundzwanzig, zweiundzwanzig...
11, 12, 13, 14, 15, 16, 17, 18, 19, 20, 21, 22...

dreissig, vierzig, fünfzig, sechzig, siebzig, achtzig, neunzig, hundert, hundertzehn, hundertelf, hundertzwölf...
30, 40, 50, 60, 70, 80, 90, 100, 110, 111, 112...

If you want to Get Your Deutsch On . . .

– You will know the meaning, the proper pronunciation, and the gender of all nouns in Lessons 2-4.
– You will know the personal pronouns in all cases.
– You will know when to use **du** and **Sie**.
– You will know personal pronouns in all genders.
– MOST IMPORTANTLY! You will know and be able to pronounce all essential phrases and vocabulary from Lessons 1-4.

Lesson 5

Essential Grammar

5.1 Declining

Taking a noun, pronoun, or adjective through all of its forms in the different cases is called "declining." Because of the work you did in Lesson 3, you know how to decline all definite articles:

Def.	m.	n.	f.	pl.
nom.	der	das	die	die
acc.	den	das	die	die
dat.	dem	dem	der	den
gen.	des	des	der	der

You also know how to decline the indefinite articles:

Indef.	m.	n.	f.	pl.
nom.	ein	ein	eine	keine
acc.	einen	ein	eine	keine
dat.	einem	einem	einer	keinen
gen.	eines	eines	einer	keiner

It would be helpful, though by no means necessary, for you to commit the two grids above to memory.

5.2 Determiners

Words like *this, that, these,* and *those* are called "determiners" in English because they help determine more specifically the meaning of the noun they refer to. They are called **Artikelwörter** in German because they act like and take the same endings as definite and indefinite articles.

5.3 Der-words

Some **Artikelwörter** are declined similarly to definite articles. We'll call these "**der**-words." Some examples are:

dieser	*this*
jeder	*every*
jener	*that*
mancher	*many a…/ some*
solcher	*such*
welcher	*which*

You can use the definite article grid above to help you decline **der**-words. For example, with **dieser**:

Def.	*m.*	*n.*	*f.*	*pl.*
nom.	dieser	dieses	diese	diese
acc.	diesen	dieses	diese	diese
dat.	diesem	diesem	dieser	diesen
gen.	dieses	dieses	dieser	dieser

Dieser Zug ist spät.
This train is late.

Fahren Sie mit diesem Zug.
Take this train.

5.3 Ein-words

Some **Artikelwörter** are declined similarly to indefinite articles. We'll call these "**ein**-words." They are mainly possessive pronouns (aka possessive adjectives) and you probably know some of them already:

mein	*my / mine*
dein	*your (sing.)*
sein	*his*
ihr	*her / their*
unser	*our*
euer	*your (pl.)*
kein	*no / none*

You can use the indefinite article grid in 5.1 to help you decline them:

Hast du mein Mofa gesehen?
Have you seen my moped?

Er hat seinen Kindern ein Meerschweinchen gegeben.
He gave his children a guinea pig.

Essential Phrases and Vocabulary

Servus!	*Hello!* (in Bavaria and Austria)
Guten Morgen! / Guten Abend!	*Good morning! / Good evening!*
Gute Nacht!	*Good night!*
Manche Leute!	*Some people!*
Ich habe eine solche Armbanduhr.	*I have a watch like that.*
In welcher Richtung ist X?	*In which direction is X?*
Wo ist deine Tasche?	*Where is your bag?*
Unsere Dusche funktioniert nicht.	*Our shower doesn't work.*
Habt ihr eure Strassenkarten?	*Do you have your street maps?*

If you want to Get Your Deutsch On . . .

– You will know the meaning, the proper pronunciation, and the gender of all nouns in Lessons 2-5.
– You will know all **der**-words and their meanings and be able to decline them.
– You will know all **ein**-words and their meanings and be able to decline them.
– MOST IMPORTANTLY! You will know and be able to pronounce all essential phrases and vocabulary from Lessons 1-5.

Lesson 6

Essential Grammar

6.1 Adjective Endings

Articles are not the only things that change in German according to case. Adjective endings also change. How they change depends on whether they follow a **der**-word, an **ein**-word, or are on their own.

Adjective endings following a definite article or **der**-word:

	m.	*n.*	*f.*	*pl.*
nom.	-e	-e	-e	-en
acc.	-en	-e	-e	-en
dat.	-en	-en	-en	-en
gen.	-en	-en	-en	-en

Das klein<u>e</u> Kind gibt jenem gross<u>en</u> Mann seinen rot<u>en</u> Fussball.
The small child gives that tall man his red football / soccer ball.

Adjective endings following an indefinite article or **ein**-word:

	m.	*n.*	*f.*	*pl.*
nom.	-er	-es	-e	-en
acc.	-en	-es	-e	-en
dat.	-en	-en	-en	-en
gen.	-en	-en	-en	-en

Ein klein<u>es</u> Kind gibt einem gross<u>en</u> Mann seinen rot<u>en</u> Fussball.
A small child gives a tall man his red soccer ball.

Adjective endings when the adjective is on its own:

	m.	n.	f.	pl.
nom.	-er	-es	-e	-e
acc.	-en	-es	-e	-e
dat.	-em	-em	-er	-en
gen.	-en	-en	-er	-er

Kleine Kinder geben grossen Frauen rote Fussbälle.
Small children give red soccer balls to tall women.

We have said it before, but it's worth repeating: Some things, while good to understand, have no bearing on your ability to understand spoken language or to make yourself understood. Adjective endings definitely fall into this category! Try to forget about them while speaking. You'll learn them naturally over time.

6.2 More Cultural Etiquette

Dinner invitations: If you're invited to someone's house for brunch or dinner, you should bring a small gift. You can never go wrong with a bouquet of flowers or a small house plant. For dinner invitations, a bottle of wine would also be fine. Or, as a foreigner, any kind of small gift from your native country would be great.

Greetings: At business and social meetings, it's common in Germany, Austria, and Switzerland to greet everyone with a firm handshake and to shake their hand again when you leave. It's important that you make eye contact when you shake hands. Greeting good friends can be slightly different. Men will shake hands when greeting and saying goodbye to male friends and acquaintances, even if they are just casually stopping to chat in the street. Close female friends, however, usually greet each other with a kiss on the cheek and again when they say goodbye. Men and women who are good friends also greet and say goodbye with a kiss on the cheek. Note: you don't actually kiss the other person's cheek, but rather touch cheeks and kiss the air beside it. The default is two kisses, one on each cheek, except in Switzerland, where they often do three. If in doubt, take your cue from the other person and remember: you can't go wrong with a handshake.

Cheers!: Whether you are in a **Kneipe** *(bar / pub)*, a restaurant, or at someone's house for dinner, if you are drinking alcohol it is important to raise your glass and wish your friends and colleagues well. Exactly what you say might depend on the situation and what part of what country you are in. Some common German expressions are **prost!** *(cheers!)* and **zum Wohl!** *(to your good health!)*, but whatever you say there are some important rules of etiquette. First, don't start drinking until you have all said cheers, not even a tiny sip. Second, make sure you touch glasses with and say cheers to every individual present. Third, make eye contact when you say cheers to people. I can not overstate how important that last rule is. Having said all of that, you still have to be practical about things. If you can't reach someone's glass because they are across the table from you, you can raise your glass towards them, but still make eye contact as you say cheers to them. If you're ever unsure of exactly what to do or say, take your cue from those around you or ask the nearest native speaker. People are usually happy to explain how things work.

Essential Phrases and Vocabulary

Woher kommst du?	*Where are you from?*
Ich komme aus den USA.	*I'm from the USA.*
Wohin gehst du?	*Where are you going?*
Ich gehe zum Bahnhof.	*I am going to the train station.*
Gibt es hier eine Kneipe?	*Is there a bar / pub here?*
Wie alt bist du?	*How old are you?*
Ich bin neunzehn Jahre alt.	*I am nineteen years old.*
Gib mir bitte das Strandtuch.	*Please hand me the beach towel.*
Nein, das grosse Strandtuch.	*No, the big beach towel.*
Mein Nachbar macht viel Lärm.	*My neighbor is very noisy.*

If you want to Get Your Deutsch On . . .

–You will know the meaning, the proper pronunciation, and the gender of all nouns in Lessons 2-6.
– You will know the adjective endings for adjectives following **der**-words, **ein**-words, and adjectives on their own.
– MOST IMPORTANTLY! You will know and be able to pronounce all essential phrases and vocabulary from Lessons 1-6.

Lesson 7

Essential Grammar

7.1 Verbs in the Present Tense

The infinitive form of a verb is its basic form. In English, this takes the form of "to…" —for example, *to run, to smoke, to write*. In German, all verbs in their infinitive form end in **-en**.

Infinitiv:	denken	machen	verkaufen	spielen
Infinitive:	*to think*	*to make / do*	*to sell*	*to play*

German verbs tend to follow a predictable pattern when we *conjugate* them in the present tense. (By "conjugate" we mean take them through their different forms for I, you, he / she / it, etc). The pattern is highlighted by the underlined endings in the following example using **spielen**:

Sing.

ich spiel<u>e</u>	*I play*
du spiel<u>st</u>	*you play*
er / sie / es spiel<u>t</u>	*he / she / it plays*

Pl.

wir spiel<u>en</u>	*we play*
ihr spiel<u>t</u>	*you play*
sie / Sie spiel<u>en</u>	*they / you (form.) play*

Verbs that follow this pattern are called "regular." Most German verbs are regular. The ones that don't follow this pattern are called "irregular."

Note: In English, we make a distinction between the present tense (e.g. *I play*) and what we call "present progressive" (e.g. *I am playing*). German does not have this distinction. The German **ich spiele** can mean both *I play* and *I am playing*. This is good news for you (one thing to learn where there were two) but not so easy for Germans leaning English (two things to learn where there was one).

7.2 Present Tense for Future Plans

We can use the present tense to talk about the future in both English and German. The future context is usually made clear by words such as "tomorrow" or "next month." For example:

Ich habe morgen Geburtstag.   *It is my birthday tomorrow.*
Wir spielen später Eishockey.   *We are playing ice hockey later.*

7.3 The Future Tense

In English we can also talk about the future with help from the verb *will*. The German verb **werden** works the exact same way. It is an irregular verb, so we need to memorize its conjugation:

Sing.		*Pl.*	
ich werde	*I will*	wir werden	*we will*
du wirst	*you will*	ihr werdet	*you will*
er / sie / es wird	*he / she / it will*	sie / Sie werden	*they / you (form.) will*

We construct the future tense in German by conjugating **werden** and using it with the infinitive of another verb, which comes at the end of the sentence:

Ich spiele Basketball.   **Ich werde morgen Basketball spielen.**
I play basketball.   *I will play basketball tomorrow.*

Ich backe Kekse.   **Ich werde am Sonntag Kekse backen.**
I am baking cookies.   *I will bake cookies on Sunday.*

Please note that the verb **werden** is also an important verb in its own right. When used on its own, it means *to become* (or *to get* in the sense of *to become*).

Ich werde müde.   **Meine Nichte wird gross.**
I am getting tired.   *My neice is getting tall.*

7.4 Haben and Sein

Haben (*to have*) and **sein** (*to be*) are two of the most important German verbs. They are not only important verbs in their own right, but we'll need their help later to talk about the past. They are both irregular, which means they don't follow the same predictable pattern we touched on in 7.1, so you should commit them to memory:

sein	to be	haben	to have
ich bin	I am	ich habe	I have
du bist	you are	du hast	you have
er / sie / es ist	he / she / it is	er / sie / es hat	he / she / it has
wir sind	we are	wir haben	we have
ihr seid	you are	ihr habt	you have
sie / Sie sind	they / you (form.) are	sie / Sie haben	they / you (form.) have

Essential Phrases and Vocabulary

Ich habe Hunger.	I am hungry.
Wir haben Durst.	We are thirsty.
Gehen wir morgen ins Kino.	Let's go to the cinema tomorrow.
Wieviel kostet das?	How much does that cost?
Es kostet zehn Euro.	It costs ten euros.
Zahlen, bitte!	We'd like to pay, please! [in a restaurant]
Spinnt ihr?	Are you (all) crazy?
Einkaufen gehen macht Spass.	Shopping is fun.
Ich liebe / hasse Tomaten.	I love / hate tomatoes.

If you want to Get Your Deutsch On . . .

– You will know the meaning, the proper pronunciation, and the gender of all nouns in Lessons 2-7.

– You will know how to conjugate any regular verb you come across in the present tense.

– You will be able to use the present tense to talk about future plans.

– You will be able to conjugate **werden** and use it to talk about the future.

– You will be able to conjugate **haben** and **sein**.

– MOST IMPORTANTLY! You will know and be able to pronounce all essential phrases and vocabulary from Lessons 1-7.

You're halfway there! Keep up the good work!

Lesson 8

Essential Grammar

8.1 Accusative Prepositions

A very loose definition of a *preposition* is that it's a short word in a sentence that tells us how a noun or pronoun in the sentence relates to something else in the sentence.

The book is on the table.

"On" is a preposition; it tells us how the book relates to the table. The book could also be under the table, or next to it, or near it, or with it, etc. German uses prepositions similarly to the way we do in English, except that German prepositions can force nouns into several different cases. We can split German prepositions into four types: accusative, dative, two-way, and genitive. There is no way to tell one type from another other than to memorize them.

The following are examples of some common accusative prepositions:

bis	*until*
durch	*through*
für	*for*
gegen	*against*
ohne	*without*
um	*until / around / at*
wider	*against / contrary to*

Das Geschenk ist für meinen Vater.
The gift is for my father.

Er geht ohne seinen Bruder.
He's going without his brother.

8.2 Dative Prepositions

The following are examples of some common <u>dative prepositions</u>:

aus	*out of*
ausser	*besides; except*
bei	*near; next to; at*
mit	*with*
nach	*to; toward; after*
seit	*since*
von	*from; of*
zu	*to; toward*

Ich fahre mit dem Fahrrad.
I am going by bike. (literally...*with the bike.*)

8.3 Two-way Prepositions

Two-way prepositions can be accusative or dative depending on how they are used. If there is movement involved, they are accusative. If there is no movement, they are dative. Some common <u>two-way prepositions</u>:

an	*at*	**über**	*over*
auf	*on*	**unter**	*under*
hinter	*behind*	**vor**	*in front of*
in	*in; into*	**zwischen**	*between*
neben	*next to*		

Movement: **Ich gehe <u>in den</u> Bahnhof.**
                        I walk into the train station.

No Movement: **Ich bin <u>in dem</u> Bahnhof.**
                        I am in the train station.

Note: whenever you have **zu dem, bei dem, von dem,** or **in dem,** you can shorten them to **zum, beim, vom,** and **im.** In addition, **zu der** can be shortened to **zur.**

8.4 Genitive Prepositions

Here are some examples of some common genitive prepositions:

statt / anstatt	*instead of*	während	*during*
ausserhalb	*outside of*	wegen	*because of*

Der Dom wird während der Renovierung geschlossen.
The cathedral will be closed during the renovation.

Er wohnt ausserhalb der Stadt.
He lives outside of the city.

Essential Phrases and Vocabulary

Wohin gehst du?	*Where are you going?*
Ich gehe zum Bahnhof.	*I am going to the train station.*
Wo seid ihr?	*Where are you (all)?*
Wir sind in der Stadtmitte.	*We are inthe city center.*
Ich gehe nach Hause.	*I am going home.*
Bis morgen!	*Till tomorrow!*
Ich esse alles ausser Salat.	*I eat everything besides salad.*
Zum Frühstück esse ich Brötchen.	*I eat rolls for breakfast.*
Das Cafe ist bei der Apotheke.	*The cafe is near the pharmacy.*
Seit gestern...	*Since yesterday...*
Das Geld liegt auf dem Tisch.	*The money is on the table.*
Ist es in der Nähe?	*Is it nearby?*
Nach links / rechts.	*(Go) Left / right.*
Geradeaus.	*Straight ahead.*
Oben / unten.	*Upstairs / downstairs.*

If you want to Get Your Deutsch On . . .

– You will know all of the accusative, dative, two-way, and genitive prepositions.
– MOST IMPORTANTLY! You will know and be able to pronounce all essential phrases and vocabulary from Lessons 1-8.

Lesson 9

Essential Grammar

9.1 The Principle Parts of a Verb

Verbs in German have three principle parts. Knowing all three helps us understand how to use verbs correctly in the present and in the past. This is similar in English. For example, you may remember learning the three principle parts of *to ring* in school as [*ring, rang, rung*]. This helped you say things correctly in the:

- present tense: *I ring the bell today.*
- past tense: *I rang the bell yesterday.*
- present perfect tense: *I have rung the bell before.*

Just as English uses the verb *have* to help make the present perfect tense (*I have rung the bell*), German also uses helping verbs. However, it has two of them: **haben** and **sein**. From now on, we'll use **(h)** to denote when haben helps a verb, and **(s)** to denote when sein helps it. We'll get to the present perfect tense (**das Perfekt**) in a moment and to the simple past (**das Präteritum**) later. For now, however, make a mental note that when you learn a German verb, you should learn all three principle parts + its helping verb:

Infinitiv	Präteritum	Perfekt	Sein / haben	Englisch
machen	machte	gemacht	(h)	*to do / make*
haben	hatte	gehabt	(h)	*to have*
sein	war	gewesen	(s)	*to be*
fahren	fuhr	gefahren	(s)	*to drive*

9.2 Weak and Strong Verbs

Verbs in English and in German fall into two broad categories in relation to their principle parts: weak and strong. Weak German verbs follow a predictable pattern, including ending in **–t** in **das Perfekt**:

Infinitiv	Präteritum	Perfekt	Sein / haben	Englisch
denken	dachte	gedacht	(h)	*to think*
lachen	lachte	gelacht	(h)	*to laugh*
kaufen	kaufte	gekauft	(h)	*to buy*
sagen	sagte	gesagt	(h)	*to say*

Strong verbs, on the other hand, don't follow a predictable pattern. They tend to end in **-en** in **das Perfekt** and you simply have to learn them as you go along:

Infinitiv	Präteritum	Perfekt	Sein / haben	Englisch
sein	war	gewesen	(s)	to be
bleiben	blieb	geblieben	(s)	to stay
werden	wurde	geworden	(s)	to become
gehen	ging	gegangen	(s)	to go / walk

Note: Thankfully, the vast majority of German verbs are weak.

9.3 The Present Perfect

Das Perfekt in German is formed exactly the same way as the present perfect in English: you conjugate the helping verb and use the principle part from **das Perfekt**. Grammar nerds note: This third principle part is confusingly called the "past participle."

sagen	to say
ich habe gesagt	I have said
du hast gesagt	you have said
er / sie / es hat gesagt	he / she / it has said

wir haben gesagt	we have said
ihr habt gesagt	you have said
sie / Sie haben gesagt	they / you (formal) have said

fahren	to drive
ich bin gegangen	I have gone
du bist gegangen	you have gone
er / sie / es ist gegangen	he / she / it has gone

wir sind gegangen	we have gone
ihr seid gegangen	you have gone
sie / Sie sind gegangen	they / you (formal) have gone

You'll notice that in **das Perfekt** in German, the past participle comes at the end of the sentence. That is a hard and fast rule! No matter what else happens in the sentence, no matter how long it gets, that past participle comes at the end in **das Perfekt**:

Ich bin gestern nach Österreich gefahren.
I drove to Austria yesterday.

Note: German speakers use **das Perfekt** to talk about the past in spoken German (as opposed to written German), which is slightly different from how we use the present perfect in English. Though we could literally translate the sentence above as "*I have driven to Austria yesterday,*" no native English speaker would ever say that. We would say "*I drove to Austria yesterday.*" The rule of thumb is if you're speaking about the past in German, use **das Perfekt**.

Essential Phrases and Vocabulary

Wir haben es gestern gemacht.	*We did it yesterday.*
Er hat sehr laut gelacht.	*He laughed very loudly.*
Wir haben Brötchen gekauft.	*We bought (bread) rolls.*
Das habe ich schon gesagt.	*I already said that.*
Wir sind nie dort gewesen.	*We have never been there.*
Ich bin zum Hotel gefahren.	*I drove to the hotel.*
Nichts ist übrig geblieben.	*Nothing was left (over).*
Sie sind schwimmen gegangen.	*They went swimming.*

If you want to Get Your Deutsch On . . .

– You will understand what the principle parts of a verb are.
– You will know the principle parts of all verbs in this lesson, along with their helping verbs.
– You will know how to form **das Perfekt**.
– MOST IMPORTANTLY! You will know and be able to pronounce all essential phrases and vocabulary from Lessons 1-9.

Lesson 10

Essential Grammar

10.1 Simple Past

The past tense in German (**das Präteritum**), sometimes also called the simple past in English, is mainly used to talk about the past in *written* German — especially in newspapers, books, and magazines. We will only touch on it briefly, as we are mainly concerned with spoken German and you already know how to use **das Perfekt** to speak about the past.

One of the few places **das Präteritum** is regularly used in spoken German is when using **haben, sein,** and **werden** as verbs in their own right (rather than as helping verbs).

Infinitiv	Präteritum	Perfect	Sein / haben	Englisch
haben	hatte	gehabt	(h)	*to have*
sein	war	gewesen	(s)	*to be*
werden	wurde	geworden	(s)	*to become*

hatte (*had*)

Sing.		*Pl.*	
ich hatte	*I had*	wir hatten	*we had*
du hattest	*you had*	ihr hattet	*you had*
er / sie / es hatte	*he / she / it had*	sie / Sie hatten	*they / you* (form.) had

war (*was*)

Sing.		*Pl.*	
ich war	*I was*	wir waren	*we were*
du warst	*you were*	ihr wart	*you were*
er / sie / es war	*he / she / it was*	sie / Sie waren	*they / you* (form.) were

wurde (*became*)

Sing.		*Pl.*	
ich wurde	*I became*	wir wurden	*we became*
du wurdest	*you became*	ihr wurdet	*you became*
er / sie / es wurde	*he / she / it became*	sie / Sie wurden	*they / you* (form.) became

10.2 Normal Word Order

German word order is a complex and varied thing. It's one of the biggest challenges for beginners, but also one of the things that ultimately makes the German language so fun and flexible. Our primary goal here is to give you an introduction to word order rather than a full analysis.

The starting point for English and German is the same. Normal word order for a statement in both languages is:

1. Subject >> 2. Verb* >> 3. Other stuff

Das Kind / wirft / den Ball.
The child / throws / the ball.

*By "verb" we mean the conjugated form of the verb. For **das Perfekt** that would be the conjugated form of **haben** or **sein**. For example:

Das Kind / hat / den Ball geworfen.
The child / threw / the ball.

10.3 Verb Second

For many reasons, including emphasis or style, German speakers often start a statement with something other than the subject. When they do, it switches the word order to:

1. Other stuff >> 2. Verb >> 3. Subject

Den Ball wirft das Kind.
The child throws the ball.

In this example, the German sentence is emphasizing that the child is throwing *the ball,* as opposed to throwing something else. Notice, however, that the word order for the English translation in both examples stays the same. We can't change the English word order without changing the meaning. *The child throws the ball* and *The ball throws the child* mean two very different things. In German, we know the ball is being thrown no matter what because it's in the accusative case (**den** Ball).

You may have noticed that the verb was the second element in both types of word order. That is a fixed and fast rule: in any statement, the verb always comes second. This is true no matter the tense. For example, look at the normal word order for a sentence in **das Perfekt**:

Das Kind <u>hat</u> dem Mann den roten Ball geworfen.
The child threw the man the red ball.

If we start the sentence with something other than the subject, the verb still comes second:

Gestern <u>hat</u> das Kind dem Mann den roten Ball geworfen.
Yesterday the child threw the man the red ball.

Essential Phrases and Vocabulary

Wohnen Sie hier?	*Do you live here?*
Sind Sie hier auf Urlaub?	*Are you here on holiday?*
Nein. Ich studiere hier.	*No. I'm studying here.*
Ja. Ich bin hier auf Urlaub.	*Yes. I'm here on vacation / holiday.*
Wie lange bleiben Sie?	*How long are you staying?*
Ich bleibe [zwei] Wochen.	*I am staying for [two] weeks.*
Du warst nicht da.	*You weren't there.*
Ich hatte kein Geld.	*I had no money.*
Die Raupe wurde zum Schmetterling.	*The caterpillar became a butterfly.*

If you want to Get Your Deutsch On . . .

– You will understand the simple past and be able to use it for **sein, haben,** and **werden.**
– You will understand normal word order and what to do when a sentence starts with something other than the subject.
– MOST IMPORTANTLY! You will know and be able to pronounce all essential phrases and vocabulary from Lessons 1-10.

Lesson 11

Essential Grammar

11.1 Modal Auxiliary Verbs

Modal auxiliary verbs are used in both German and English to express ability, likelihood, permission, etc. English modal verbs include *can, may, want, should, must,* and *like.* The German modals are:

Infinitiv	Präteritum	Perfekt	Sein / haben	Englisch
können	konnte	gekonnt	(h)	*can*
dürfen	durfte	gedurft	(h)	*may*
wollen	wollte	gewollt	(h)	*want*
sollen	sollte	gesollt	(h)	*should*
müssen	musste	gemusst	(h)	*must*
mögen	mochte	gemocht	(h)	*like*

In German, we conjugate the modal verb and use it with the infinitive of another verb, which always comes at the end of the sentence:

Wir können das machen.   **Das sollen wir nicht sagen.**
We can do that.   *We shouldn't say that.*

German modal verbs are all irregular, but as a group their conjugation follows a pattern of sorts. Here is the present tense conjugation:

Infinitiv	ich	du	er/sie/es	wir	ihr	sie / Sie
können	kann	kannst	kann	können	könnt	können
dürfen	darf	darfst	darf	dürfen	dürft	dürfen
wollen	will	willst	will	wollen	wollt	wollen
sollen	soll	sollst	soll	sollen	sollt	sollen
müssen	muss	musst	muss	müssen	müsst	müssen
mögen	mag	magst	mag	mögen	mögt	mögen

In Section 10.1 we said that with few exceptions **das Präteritum** is rarely used in spoken German to talk about the past. Modal verbs constitute one of those exceptions:

Ich konnte die Kneipe nicht finden.
I couldn't find the bar / pub.

Ich wollte mitkommen, durfte aber nicht.
I wanted to come with, but wasn't allowed to.

11.2 Man kann...

In spoken English there are lots of ways of asking or talking about how one does something in general. For example, we can ask: *How does one...? How do you...? How does a person...?* Most of those are expressed in German using the pronoun **man** *(you / one)*. It's used in the third person singular (**er / sie / es** form) and isn't capitalized, except at the beginning of a sentence:

Kann man in der Nähe parken?
Can you park nearby?

Wie sagt man das auf Deutsch?
How do you say that in German?

Man darf das hier nicht machen.
You aren't allowed to do that here.

Wie kommt man am besten zum Kino / Strand / Restaurant?
What's the best way to get to the cinema / beach / restaurant?

11.3 Compound Verbs

We won't delve too deeply into compound verbs, but you should at least be aware that they exist. They are formed in German by combining a "normal" verb you may already be familiar with and a prefix, such as **ab-, an-, ver-, aus-**, etc. The hard part is that some prefixes separate ("seperable prefixes") and move to the end of the sentence when you conjugate them in the present tense. Some, however, don't ("inseperable prefixes"). You can find long lists of the seperable vs. inseperable prefixes online. The good news is that whether seperable or not, you simply conjugate the main verb:

The verb **ankommen** (*to arrive*) is separable; **verstehen** (*to understand*) is not.

Wann kommt der Zug an? Er kommt erst morgen an.
When does the train arrive? It doesn't arrive until tomorrow.

Ich verstehe nicht.
I don't understand.

Compound verbs are also sometimes formed together with nouns or other verbs and behave in the same way as **ankommen** (i.e. seperable). For example, *to ride a bicycle* is **Rad fahren** and *to go shopping* is **einkaufen gehen**.

Wir fahren fast nie Rad.
We almost never ride our bikes.

Wir gehen im Supermarkt einkaufen.
We are going shopping in the supermarket.

Essential Phrases and Vocabulary

Wir müssen die Karten abholen.	*We have to pick up the tickets.*
Könnt ihr die Bühne sehen?	*Can you see the stage?*
Wir wollen tanzen!	*We want to dance!*
Ich mag diese Stadt!	*I like this city!*
Sie hat viel anzubieten!	*It has a lot to offer!*
Wir sollen nach Hause gehen.	*We should go home.*
Darf ich Ihren Kuli benutzen?	*May I use your pen?*
Wann fängt das Spiel an?	*When does the game / match start?*

If you want to Get Your Deutsch On . . .

– You will know the modal auxiliary verbs in the present tense (and maybe even in the past)!
– You will understand how to use the pronoun **man**.
– You will have a basic overview of compound verbs.
– MOST IMPORTANTLY! You will know and be able to pronounce all essential phrases and vocabulary from Lessons 1-11.

Lesson 12

Essential Grammar

12.1 Questions without Question Words

In both German and English you can ask a question simply by reversing the subject and verb:

Wir fahren zum Flughafen.
We are driving to the airport.

Fahren wir zum Flughafen?
Are we driving to the airport?

Sie sind gestern mit dem Taxi zum Flughafen gefahren.
They took a taxi to the airport yesterday.

Sind sie gestern mit dem Taxi zum Flughafen gefahren?
Did they take a taxi to the airport yesterday?

12.1 Questions with Question Words

As in English, you can ask questions in German using question words:

wann	*when*
warum	*why*
was	*what*
wer	*who*
wie	*how*
wo	*where*
wohin	*where to* (like the old-fashioned *whither*)
wovon	*where from* (like the old-fashioned *whence*)

Just as in English, when you start a sentence with a question word, the verb comes next:

Warum tut er das?	*Why does he do that?*
Was gibt es zum Abendessen?	*What's for dinner?*
Wer fehlt noch?	*Who is still missing?*
Wie soll ich das wissen?	*How should I know that?*
Wo bleibt Michael?	*Where is Michael?*

12.2 Liking Things

There are several ways of "liking" things in German: **mögen** *(to like)*, **möchten** *(would like)*, **etwas gern haben** *(to like / enjoy something)*, and **einem etwas gefallen** *(to find something pleasing)*.

<u>Mögen</u>
We looked at **mögen** in the last lesson on modal verbs:

Ich mag das nicht.
I don't like that.

<u>Möchten</u>
Möchten means "would like" and is related to **mögen**. It should be treated like a modal verb and is conjugated as follows:

Sing.

ich möchte	*I would like*
du möchtest	*you would like*
er / sie / es möchte	*he / she / it would like*

Pl.

wir möchten	*we would like*
ihr möchtet	*you would like*
sie / Sie möchten	*they would like*

Welches Eis möchtest du?
Which ice cream would you like?

Ich möchte zum Hotel gehen.
I would like to go to the hotel.

<u>Etwas gern haben</u>
This behaves like a seperable prefix verb:

Ich habe Kekse / Müsli / Martinis (nicht) gern.
I (don't) like cookies / muesli / martinis.

If you're talking about something you enjoy doing, you can simply use the verb you enjoy doing and add **gern** at the end:

Ich laufe / schwimme / esse gern.
I enjoy running / swimming / eating.

<u>Gefallen</u>

Gefallen is usually translated as *to like*, but it can help to think of it as *to find something pleasing*. It's a dative verb.

Gefallen dir Blumen? Ja, Blumen gefallen mir.
Do you like flowers? Yes, I like flowers.

Essential Phrases and Vocabulary

Wohin gehst du?	*Where are you going?*
Ich gehe zum Hauptbahnhof.	*I am going to the main train station.*
Gehen wir!	*Let's go!*
Gibt es eine Kneipe in der Gegend?	*Is there a bar / pub nearby?*
Wo steht das Auto?	*Where is the car?*
Hier!	*Here!*
Dort!	*There!*
Es ist nicht weit.	*It is not far.*
Rechts.	*Right.*
Links.	*Left.*
Geradeaus.	*Straight ahead.*
Was ist los?	*What's wrong?*
Nichts! Ich habe Langeweile!	*Nothing! I'm bored!*
Machen wir etwas aufregendes!	*Let's do something exciting!*
Wo?	*Where?*
Ja, Wien natürlich!	*Vienna, of course!*
Was machen wir dort?	*What will we do there?*
Kaiserschmarrn essen.	*Eat kaiserschmarrn.*

If you want to Get Your Deutsch On . . .

– You will be able to ask questions with and without question words.
– You will know several different ways to express a like or dislike for things.
– MOST IMPORTANTLY! You will know and be able to pronounce all essential phrases and vocabulary from Lessons 1-12.

Lesson 13

Essential Grammar

13.1 Coordinating Conjunctions

Coordinating conjunctions are used to connect thoughts, phrases, ideas, or sentences that are more or less similar. The main ones in English are *but*, *or*, and *and*. The main ones in German are:

denn	*because*
aber	*but*
oder	*or*
und	*and*
sondern	*(but) rather*

The great thing about coordinating conjunctions in German is that they do not affect the normal word order of either part of the sentence:

Ich bin nicht zum Konzert gegangen, denn ich kann Ska nicht leiden.
I didn't go to the concert because I can't stand ska music.

Ich wollte mitgehen, aber ich war zu spät.
I wanted to go along, but I was too late.

Wir können ins Kino gehen, oder wir können zur Diskothek gehen.
We can go to the cinema, or we can go to the (night) club.

Ihr dürft eine Nachspeise und eine Käseplatte haben.
You (all) may have a dessert and a cheese board.

Ich gehe nicht schwimmen, sondern ich gehe Wasserskifahren!
I am not going swimming, but rather water skiing!

13.2 Subordinating Conjunctions

Subordinating conjunctions also connect thoughts, phrases, ideas, or sentences, but the parts are not considered equal. One part is dependent on the other. English examples of subordinating conjunctions are *after*, *although*, *if*, etc. A few common ones in German are:

weil	because
dass	*that*
wenn	*if*
ob	*whether*
obwohl	*although*

Unlike coordinating conjunctions, subordinating conjunctions affect word order. In the part of the sentence where the conjunction is located, the conjugated part of the verb comes at the end:

Ich bin nicht zum Konzert gegangen, weil ich Ska nicht leiden kann.
I didn't go to the concert because I can't stand ska music.

Ich wusste nicht, dass ich zu spät war.
I didn't know that I was too late.

Ich möchte nur ins Kino gehen, wenn ich „den Paten" anschauen darf.
I only want to go to the cinema if I can watch "The Godfather."

Ich habe nicht gefragt, ob es eine Käseplatte gibt.
I haven't asked whether there is a cheese board.

Ich kann nicht schwimmen, obwohl ich Wasserskifahren kann.
I can't swim, although I can water ski.

If you start a sentence with a subordinating conjunction, it affects the word order in both parts of the sentence. The first part will be as we just described (verb at the end) and the second part will have the verb at the beginning:

Obwohl ich Wasserskifahren kann, kann ich nicht schwimmen.
Although I can water ski, I can't swim.

A few things to note:

1) The portion of the sentence which starts with the subordinating conjunction is called a "subordinate clause."

2) A subordinate clause is not a sentence in its own right and serves to emphasize the other part of the sentence, the "main clause," which is a sentence in its own right.

3) Our verb second rule from 10.3 still applies (1. Other stuff >> 2. Verb >> 3. Subject). In the example above, the entire subordinate clause is "other stuff" >> **kann** is the verb >> **ich** is the subject.

Don't worry if you find the grammatical workings of subordinate clauses confusing. You don't need to understand the grammar to use them. Though they seem complicated, they are used a lot in everyday speech, so you'll hear plenty of examples and have plenty of opportunities to practice. And, as we have said many times before, getting it wrong won't affect your ability to make yourself understood!

Essential Phrases and Vocabulary

Darf ich mit Kreditkarte bezahlen?	*May I pay by credit card?*
Nein, wir akzeptieren nur Bargeld.	*No, we only take cash.*
Wo ist die Apotheke?	*Where is the pharmacy?*
Gleich um die Ecke.	*Right around the corner.*
Fühlst du dich unwohl?	*Do you feel unwell?*
Ja, ich habe Kopfschmerzen.	*Yes, I have a headache.*
Ich habe mich verlaufen!	*I am lost!*
Wo ist die nächste U-bahnstation?	*Where is the nearest subway / metro/ tube station?*
Der Polizeiwache gegenüber.	*Across from the police station.*
Eine Einzelfahrkarte nach X, bitte.	*A single ticket to X, please.*

If you want to Get Your Deutsch On . . .

– You will know the coordinating and subordinating conjunctions in this lesson and how to use them.

– MOST IMPORTANTLY! You will know and be able to pronounce all essential phrases and vocabulary from Lessons 1-13.

Lesson 14

Essential Grammar

14.1 Days of the Week and Months of the Year

Montag	*Monday*
Dienstag	*Tuesday*
Mittwoch	*Wednesday*
Donnerstag	*Thursday*
Freitag	*Friday*
Samstag	*Saturday*
Sonntag	*Sunday*

All of the days of the week are masculine (**der**) and as in English, there are three main ways you will say them:

On their own
Dienstag ist der zweite Tag der Woche.
Tuesday is the second day of the week.

With the word "on"
Am Mittwoch fliege ich nach Paris.
On Wednesday I am flying to Paris.

As part of something recurring
Freitags spiele ich immer Fussball!
Fridays I always play soccer / football!

The months of the year are **Januar, Februar, März, April, Mai, Juni, Juli, August, September, Oktober, November,** and **Dezember.** They are all masculine.

Im Januar habe ich Geburtstag! Wann hast du Geburtstag?
My birthday is in January! When is your birthday?

14.2 The Date

To say the date you'll need to know the ordinal numbers (the irregular ones have been highlighted):

Numeral	Cardinal	Ordinal
0	null	
1	eins	erste
2	zwei	zweite
3	drei	dritte
4	vier	vierte
5	fünf	fünfte
6	sechs	sechste
7	sieben	siebte
8	acht	achte
9	neun	neunte
10	zehn	zehnte
11	elf	elfte
12	zwölf	zwölfte
13	dreizehn	dreizehnte
14	vierzehn	vierzehnte
15	fünfzehn	fünfzehnte
16	sechzehn	sechzehnte
17	siebzehn	siebzehnte
18	achtzehn	achtzehnte
19	neunzehn	neunzehnte
20	zwanzig	zwanzigste (-ste from here on)
30	dreissig	dreissigste

Ordinal numbers are adjectives, so their endings will change according to how they are used. Also, just as you can write *twentieth* as "20th" in English, you can write **zwanzigste(n) as "20."** in German.

Nom.	**der zwanzigste Januar (der 20. Januar)**
Acc.	**den zwanzigsten Januar (den 20. Januar)**
Dat.	**dem zwanzigsten Januar (dem 20. Januar)**

Der zwanzigste Januar ist übermorgen.
The twentieth of January is the day after tomorrow.

Welches Datum haben wir heute?
What's the date today?

Heute haben wir den 15. Januar. Am 20. habe ich Geburtstag!
Today is the 15ᵗʰ of January. The 20th is my birthday!

14.3 Telling Time

German speakers use a 24-hour clock.

Wieviel Uhr ist es?	**Es ist acht Uhr.**
What time is it?	*It is 8 o'clock.*

To keep things simple, it's perfectly acceptable to state the time as you would read a digital clock:

Es ist acht Uhr zehn.	**Es ist acht Uhr fünfundvierzig.**
It is eight ten.	*It is eight forty-five.*

Essential Phrases and Vocabulary

Morgen ist mein letzter Tag hier.	*Tommorow is my last day here.*
Ich möchte nicht gehen.	*I don't want to go.*
Bleiben wir in Kontakt.	*Let's stay in touch.*
Auf Wiedersehen!	*Goodbye!*
Wann fahren wir ab?	*When do we depart?*
jetzt / heute / gestern	*now / today / yesterday*
heute morgen / abend	*this morning / evening*
diese Woche	*this week*
Wo / wann treffen wir uns?	*Where / when will we meet?*
Treffen wir uns um acht Uhr.	*Let's meet at eight o'clock.*
Treffen wir uns am Flughafen.	*Let's meet at the airport.*
Bist du bereit? Ich bin bereit!	*Are you ready? I am ready!*
Bis bald!	*See you soon!*

If you want to Get Your Deutsch On . . .

– You will know how to use the days of the week and months of the year.
– You will know how to ask the date and the time.
– MOST IMPORTANTLY! You will know and be able to pronounce all essential phrases and vocabulary from Lessons 1-14.

Part Two. The Glossary

Essential Vocabulary

The following glossary contains all the German words used in this book and many more that you might find useful. All German verbs list all three principle parts and the helping verb: (h) for haben and (s) for sein (see Lesson 9 for more detail). All German nouns have the corresponding article (der, die or das), as well as the plural ending. Using the examples from Lesson 2.3, here is how plurals are noted in the glossary:

Plural ending	Singular / Plural	Glossary entry
-n	die Katze / die Katzen	die Katze, -n
-e	der Wein / die Weine	der Wein, -e
-s	das Auto / die Autos	das Auto, -s
¨er	das Buch / die Bücher	das Buch, ¨er
No change	das Mädchen / die Mädchen	das Mädchen, -

GERMAN—ENGLISH

A

abend	evening
das Abendessen, -	dinner
aber	but
alt	old
anbieten (bot an, angeboten) (h)	to offer
anfangen (fing an, angefangen) (h)	to begin
anschauen (schaute an, angeschaut) (h)	to look at; watch
der Apfel, ¨	apple
die Apotheke, -n	chemist; pharmacy
die Armbanduhr, -en	wristwatch
auch	also
auf	on
Auf Wiedersehen!	Goodbye!
aus	out; out of
ausser	besides; except
ausserhalb	outside of
Australien	Australia
das Auto, -s	car

B

der Bahnhof, ¨e	train station
bald	soon
der Ball, ¨e	ball
die Bank, -en	bank (financial)

das Bargeld, -er — cash
bedeuten (bedeutete, bedeutet) (h) — to mean
bei — near; next to; at
bereit — ready
das Bier, -e — beer
bis — until
bitte — please
schwarz — black
bleiben (blieb, geblieben) (s) — stay
die Blume, -n — flower
das Brötchen, - — roll (i.e. bread roll)
das Brot, -e — bread
der Bruder, ⁚ — brother
die Bühne, -n — stage (noun)

C
No German entries.

D
das Datum, die Daten — date (as in calendar)
decken (deckte, gedeckt) (h) — to set (e.g. *to set the table*)
dein — your (sing.)
denken (dachte, gedacht) (h) — to think
denn — because (coordinating conj.)
deutsch — German (adjective)
das Deutsch (no plural) — German (the language)
Deutschland — Germany
die Sprache, -n — language
der Dienstag, -e — Tuesday
dieser — this
die Disko, -s — club (with music and dancing)
der Donnerstag, -e — Thursday
dort — there
dumm — dumb
durch — through
dürfen (durfte, gedurft) (h) — may
die Dusche, -n — shower (noun)

E
die Ecke, -n — corner
ein — one
einkaufen (kaufte ein, eingekauft) (h) — to shop
englisch — English (adjective)
das Englisch (no plural) — English (the language)

Entschuldigung!	excuse me / pardon me!
etwas gern tun (tat, getan) (h)	enjoy doing something
euer	your (pl.)

F

fahren (fuhr, gefahren) (s)	drive
die Fahrkarte, -n	ticket (for travel)
das Fahrrad, ⁝er	bike (noun)
die Familie, -n	family
fliegen (flog, geflogen) (s)	to fly
der Flughafen, ⁝	airport
die Frage, -n	question
fragen (fragte, gefragt) (h)	to ask
der Freitag, -e	Friday
der Freund, -e	friend
das Frühstück, -e	breakfast
früh	early
funktionieren (funktionierte, funktioniert) (h)	to function
für	for
der Fussball, ⁝e	football; soccer

G

der Geburtstag	birthday
gegen	against
die Gegend, -en	vicinity; area; neighborhood
gehen (ging, gegangen) (s)	to go
das Geld, -er	money
geradeaus	straight ahead
das Geschenk, -e	gift; present
gestern	yesterday
gross	big; tall
Grossbritanien	Great Britain
gut	good
haben (hatte, gehabt) (h)	to have

H

das Handy, -s	cell phone; mobile phone
das Haus, ⁝er	house
heissen (hiess, geheissen) (h)	to be called; named
heute	today
hier	here
hinter	behind
das Hotel, -s	hotel

I

ich	I
ihr	her
in	in; into
Irland	Ireland

J

ja	yes
das Jahr, -e	year
jeder	every
jener	that
jetzt	now
jung	young

K

der Kaffee, -	coffee
Kanada	Canada
die Karte, -n	ticket; map
die Katze, -n	cat
kaufen (kaufte, gekauft) (h)	to buy
kein	no / none
der Keks, -e	cookie
das Kino, -s	cinema; movie theater
klein	little; small
das Kleingeld (no plural)	change (as in coins)
das Klo, -s	toilet; restroom
die Kneipe, -n	bar; pub
die Konditorei, -en	pastry shop
können (konnte, gekonnt) (h)	can / to be able to
das Konzert, -e	concert
der Kopfschmerz, -en	headache
kosten (kostete, gekostet) (h)	to cost
die Kreditkarte, n	credit card
die Kusine, -n	cousin (female)

L

lachen (lachte, gelacht) (h)	to laugh
laut	loud
leise	quiet
links	left

M

machen (machte, gemacht) (h)	to make
das Mädchen, -	girl
mancher	many a… / some
der Mann, ̈er	man
die Mehrzahl, -en	plural
mein	my
mit	with
der Mittwoch, -e	Wednesday
möchten (present tense only)	would like
das Mofa, -s	moped
mögen (mochte, gemocht) (h)	to like
der Monat, -e	month
der Montag, -e	Monday
der Morgen, -	morning
das Müsli, -	muesli
müssen (musste, gemusst) (h)	must
die Mutter, ̈	mother

N

nach	to; toward; after
nach Hause gehen	go home
der Nachbar	neighbor
der Nachmittag, -e	afternoon
die Nachspeise, -n	dessert
die Nacht, ̈e	night
der Name, -n	name (noun)
neben	next to
nein	no
Neuseeland	New Zealand
nicht	not
nie	never
nochmal	again
Nordirland	Northern Ireland
nur	only

O

ob	whether
obwohl	although
oder	or
ohne	without
Österreich	Austria
österreichisch	Austrian

P

parken (parkte, geparkt) (h)	to park
das Perfekt	present perfect tense
pflücken (pflückte, gepflückt) (h)	to pick (e.g. flowers)
die Polizei	police
die Polizeiwache, -n	police station
das Präteritum	past (grammatical)

R

Rad fahren (fuhr Rad, Rad gefahren) (s)	to cycle; to ride a bicycle
rechts	right
die Reise, -n	journey; trip
das Restaurant, -e	restaurant
die Richtung, -en	direction
rot	red

S

sagen (sagte, gesagt) (h)	to say
der Salat, -e	salad
das Salz, -	salt
der Samstag, -e	Saturday
satt	full (full stomach)
sauber	clean (adjective)
der Schlüssel, -	key
der Schmetterling, -e	butterfly
schnell	quick; fast
die Schokolade, -n	chocolate
schon	already
schön	pretty
Schottland	Scotland
schreiben (schrieb, geschrieben) (h)	to write
die Schweiz	Switzerland
schweizerisch	Swiss
die Schwester, -	sister
schwierig	difficult
schwimmen (schwamm, geschwommen) (s)	to swim
sein	his
sein (war, gewesen) (s)	to be
seit	since
solcher	such
sollen (sollte, gesollt) (h)	should
der Sonntag, -e	Sunday
sondern	but rather

spät	late
später	later
das Spiel, -e	game; match
spinnen (spann, gesponnen) (h)	to be crazy
spielen (spielte, gespielt) (h)	to play
sprechen (sprach, gesprochen) (h)	to speak
die Stadt, ¨e	city
die Stadtmitte, -n	city center
statt / anstatt	instead of
der Strand, ¨e	beach
studieren (studierte, studiert) (h)	to study
Südafrika	South Africa
der Supermarkt, ¨e	super market

T

der Tag, -e	day
tanzen (tanzte, getanzt) (h)	to dance
die Tasche, n	bag
das Taxi, -s	taxi
der Tee, -s	tea
der Tisch, -e	table
die Toilette, -n	toilet
trinken (trank, getrunken) (h)	to drink

U

über	over
um	around; at; until
und	and
unser	our
unter	under
unwohl	unwell
der Urlaub, -e	holiday; vacation
die USA	USA

V

der Vater, ¨	father
die Vereinigten Staaten von Amerika	The United States of America
das Vereinigte Königreich	The United Kingdom
die Vergangenheit, -en	past (historical)
verkaufen (verkaufte, verkauft) (h)	to sell
verstehen (verstand, verstanden) (h)	to understand
der Vetter, -	cousin (male)
viel	many

| von | from; of |
| vor | in front of |

W

während	during
Wales	Wales
wann	when
warum	why
was	what
das Wasser, -	water
weder...noch	neither...nor
wegen	because of
weil	because
der Wein, -e	wine
weit	far
welcher	which
wenn	if
wer	who
werden (wurde, geworden) (s)	to become
werfen (warf, geworfen) (h)	to throw
wider	contrary to
wie	how
wieder	again
Wien	Vienna
wir	we
wissen (wusste, gewusst) (h)	to know
wo	where
die Woche, -n	week
woher	where from
wohin	where to
wohnen (wohnte, gewohnt) (h)	to live (e.g. *to live in New York*)
wollen (wollte, gewollt) (h)	to want
die Wurst, ⁻e	sausage

X, Y

No German entries.

Z

der Zebrastreifen, -	zebra crossing; pedestrian crossing
das Zimmer, -	room
der Zoo, -s	zoo
zu	to; toward
der Zug, ⁻e	train (noun)
zwischen	between

ENGLISH-GERMAN

A

after	nach
afternoon	der Nachmittag, -e
again	wieder; nochmal
against	gegen
airport	der Flughafen, ⁻
already	schon
also	auch
although	obwohl
and	und
apple	der Apfel, ⁻
around	um
to ask	fragen (fragte, gefragt) (h)
at	um
Australia	Australien
Austria	Österreich
Austrian	österreichisch

B

bag	die Tasche, n
ball	der Ball, ⁻e
bank (financial)	die Bank, -en
bar	die Kneipe, -n
to be	sein (war, gewesen) (s)
beach	der Strand, ⁻e
because	denn; weil
because of	wegen
to become	werden (wurde, geworden) (s)
beer	das Bier, -e
to begin	anfangen (fing an, angefangen) (h)
behind	hinter
besides; except	ausser
between	zwischen
big	gross
bike (noun)	das Fahrrad, ⁻er
birthday	der Geburtstag
bread	das Brot, -e
breakfast	das Frühstück, -e
brother	der Bruder, ⁻

but	aber
but rather	sondern
butterfly	der Schmetterling, -e

C

can	können (konnte, gekonnt) (h)
Canada	Kanada
car	das Auto, -s
cash	das Bargeld, -er
cat	die Katze, -n
cell phone	das Handy, -s
change (e.g. *loose change*)	das Kleingeld (no plural)
chemist	die Apotheke, -n
chocolate	die Schokolade, -n
cinema	das Kino, -s
city	die Stadt, ¨e
clean (adjective)	sauber
city center	die Stadtmitte, -n
club (with music and dancing)	die Disko, -s
coffee	der Kaffee, -
concert	das Konzert, -e
contrary to	wider
cookie	der Keks, -e
corner	die Ecke, -n
to cost	kosten (kostete, gekostet) (h)
cousin (female)	die Kusine, -n
cousin (male)	der Vetter, -
to be crazy	spinnen (spann, gesponnen) (h)
credit card	die Kreditkarte, -n
to cycle	Rad fahren (fuhr Rad, Rad gefahren) (s)

D

to dance	tanzen (tanzte, getanzt) (h)
date (as in calendar)	das Datum, die Daten
day	der Tag, -e
dessert	die Nachspeise, -n
difficult	schwierig
dinner	das Abendessen, -
direction	die Richtung, -en
to drink	trinken (trank, getrunken) (h)
to drive	fahren (fuhr, gefahren) (s)
dumb	dumm
during	während

E

early	früh
English (adjective)	englisch
English (the language)	das Englisch (no plural)
to enjoy doing something	etwas gern tun (tat, getan) (h)
evening	abend
every	jeder
Excuse me! / Pardon me!	Entschuldigung!

F

family	die Familie, -n
far	weit
father	der Vater, ᷉
flower	die Blume, -n
fly	fliegen (flog, geflogen) (s)
football	der Fussball, ᷉e
for	für
friend	der Freund, -e
Friday	der Freitag, -e
from; of	von
full (full stomach)	satt
to function	funktionieren (funktionierte, funktioniert) (h)

G

game	das Spiel, -e
gift	das Geschenk, -e
girl	das Mädchen, -
good	gut
Germany	Deutschland
German (adjective)	deutsch
German (the language)	das Deutsch (no plural)
to go	gehen (ging, gegangen) (s)
to go home	nach Hause gehen
Goodbye!	Auf Wiedersehen!
Great Britain	Grossbritannien

H

to have	haben (hatte, gehabt) (h)
headache	der Kopfschmerz, -en
here	hier
her	ihr
his	sein
holiday	der Urlaub, -e

hotel	das Hotel, -s
house	das Haus, ¨er
how	wie

I

I	ich
if	wenn
in front of	vor
in; into	in
instead of	statt / anstatt
Ireland	Irland

J

journey	die Reise, -n

K

key	der Schlüssel, -
to know	wissen (wusste, gewusst) (h)

L

language	die Sprache, -n
late	spät
later	später
to laugh	lachen (lachte, gelacht) (h)
left	links
to like	mögen (mochte, gemocht) (h)
little	klein
to live (e.g. *to live in New York*)	wohnen (wohnte, gewohnt) (h)
to look at	anschauen (schaute an, angeschaut) (h)
loud	laut

M

to make	machen (machte, gemacht) (h)
man	der Mann, ¨er
many	viel
many a... / some	mancher
may	dürfen (durfte, gedurft) (h)
to mean	bedeuten (bedeutete, bedeutet) (h)
mobile phone	das Handy, -s
Monday	der Montag, -e
money	das Geld, -er
month	der Monat, -e
moped	das Mofa, -s

morning	der Morgen, -
mother	die Mutter, ¨
movie theater	das Kino, -s
muesli	das Müsli, -
must	müssen (musste, gemusst) (h)
my	mein

N

name	der Name, -n
to be called / named	heissen (hiess, geheissen) (h)
near; next to; at	bei
neighbor	der Nachbar
neither...nor	weder...noch
never	nie
New Zealand	Neuseeland
next to	neben
night	die Nacht, ¨e
no	nein
no / none	kein
Northern Ireland	Nordirland
not	nicht
now	jetzt

O

to offer	anbieten (bot an, angeboten) (h)
old	alt
on	auf
one	ein
only	nur
or	oder
our	unser
out; out of	aus
outside of	ausserhalb
over	über

P

to park	parken (parkte, geparkt) (h)
past (grammatical)	das Präteritum
past (historical)	die Vergangenheit, -en
pastry shop	die Konditorei, -en
pedestrian crossing	der Zebrastreifen, -
pharmacy	die Apotheke, -n
to pick (e.g. flowers)	pflücken (pflückte, gepflückt) (h)

to play	spielen (spielte, gespielt) (h)
please	bitte
plural	die Mehrzahl, -en
police	die Polizei
police station	die Polizeiwache, -n
present (e.g. birthday present)	das Geschenk, -e
present perfect tense	das Perfekt
pretty	schön
pub	die Kneipe, -n

Q

question	die Frage, -n
quick	schnell
quiet	leise

R

ready	bereit
red	rot
restaurant	das Restaurant, -s
right	rechts
roll (i.e. bread roll)	das Brötchen, -
room	das Zimmer, -

S

salad	der Salat, -e
salt	das Salz, -e
Saturday	der Samstag, -e
sausage	die Wurst, ¨e
to say	sagen (sagte, gesagt) (h)
black	schwarz
Scotland	Schottland
to sell	verkaufen (verkaufte, verkauft) (h)
to set (e.g. to set the table)	decken (deckte, gedeckt) (h)
to shop	einkaufen (kaufte ein, eingekauft) (h)
should	sollen (sollte, gesollt) (h)
shower (noun)	die Dusche, -n
since	seit
sister	die Schwester, -n
small	klein
soccer	der Fussball, ¨e
soon	bald
South Africa	Südafrika
to speak	sprechen (sprach, gesprochen) (h)

stage (noun)	die Bühne, -n
to stay	bleiben (blieb, geblieben) (s)
straight ahead	geradeaus
to study	studieren (studierte, studiert) (h)
such	solcher
Sunday	der Sonntag, -e
super market	der Supermarkt, ¨e
to swim	schwimmen (schwamm, geschwommen) (s)
Swiss	schweizerisch
Switzerland	die Schweiz

T

table	der Tisch, -e
tall	gross
taxi	das Taxi, -s
tea	der Tee, -s
that	jener
there	dort
to think	denken (dachte, gedacht) (h)
this	dieser
through	durch
to throw	werfen (warf, geworfen) (h)
Thursday	der Donnerstag, -e
ticket	die Karte, -n
ticket (for travel)	die Fahrkarte, -n
to; toward	zu
to; toward; after	nach
today	heute
toilet	die Toilette, -n; das Klo,-s
train (noun)	der Zug, ¨e
train station	der Bahnhof, ¨e
Tuesday	der Dienstag, -e

U

under	unter
to understand	verstehen (verstand, verstanden) (h)
The United Kingdom	das Vereinigte Königreich
The United States of America	die Vereinigten Staaten von Amerika
until	bis; um
unwell	unwohl
USA	die USA

V

vacation	der Urlaub, -e
vicinity	die Gegend, -en
Vienna	Wien

W

Wales (the country)	Wales
to want	wollen (wollte, gewollt) (h)
water	das Wasser, ∷
we	wir
Wednesday	der Mittwoch, -e
week	die Woche, -n
what	was
when	wann
where	wo
where from	woher
where to	wohin
whether	ob
which	welcher
who	wer
why	warum
wine	der Wein, -e
with	mit
without	ohne
would like	möchten (present tense only)
wristwatch	die Armbanduhr, -en
to write	schreiben (schrieb, geschrieben) (h)

Y

year	das Jahr, -e
yes	ja
yesterday	gestern
young	jung
your (pl.)	euer
your (sing.)	dein

Z

zoo	der Zoo, -s
zebra crossing	der Zebrastreifen, -

Further Reading and Learning

When you're ready to take the plunge into more advanced German, there are many useful guides that can be found on the internet. It's difficult to recommend one in particular because there are so many and everyone needs to find the one that suits their particular learning style or has good explanations of information they are after. One indispensable online tool I would recommend, however, is LEO (http://www.leo.org/englisch-deutsch/), a free-to-use online English<>German dictionary created by the University of Munich with pronunciation audio clips for every word.

While online, don't forget about music. You will be amazed at how powerful music can be for learning a foreign language. Simply print out the lyrics to your favorite German song and practice singing along. If you don't have a favorite German song, try a few hits from the 1980s, such as "99 Luftballoons" by Nena and "Männer" by Herbert Grönemeyer.

For the grammar nerds among you, I'd strongly recommend the following book:

Dreyer, Hilke. 2015. *Lehr- und Übungsbuch der deutschen Grammatik—Aktuell.* (Ismaning: Max Hueber Verlag).

Formal language instruction is obviously a great way to learn a language. For those of you who are based in the U.S., The Concordia Language Villages, located in the north woods of Minnesota, is a great place to start for children, adults, and families alike. The German village is called *Waldsee* and you are guaranteed to have a wonderful time learning German in beautiful surroundings.

If you want to immerse yourself in language study in Germany, then the Goethe Institut has excellent language schools all over the world (www.goethe.de). Or, you can be daring and simply travel to Germany, Austria, or German-speaking Switzerland and learn by mixing with the locals.

Wherever your German language journey takes you, ich und Theran Press wünschen euch allen viel Spass auf der Reise!

www.ingramcontent.com/pod-product-compliance
Lightning Source LLC
LaVergne TN
LVHW041326080426
835513LV00008B/605